A New True Book

WORLD'S FAIRS AND EXPOS

By Allan Fowler

CHILDRENS PRESS ®
CHICAGO

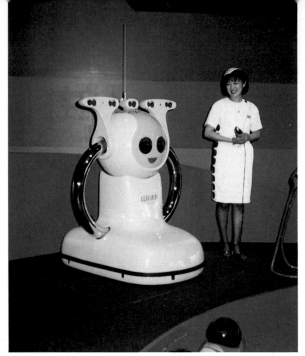

Robot "actor," Fuyo Robot Theater.
Expo '85, Tsukuba, Japan, 1985

Library of Congress Cataloging-in-Publication Data

Fowler, Allan.
　World's fairs and expos / by Allan Fowler.
　　p.　　cm. — (A New true book)
　Includes index.
　Summary: Describes historic and modern world's fairs, where new and future inventions, and styles of architecture, art, and entertainment are previewed.
　ISBN 0-516-01130-8
　1.　Exhibitions—Juvenile literature.
[1.　Exhibitions.]　I.　Title.
T395.F68　1991　　　　　　　91-8891
907.4—dc20　　　　　　　　　CIP
　　　　　　　　　　　　　　AC

TABLE OF CONTENTS

What Is an Expo?...5

Inside the Pavilions...8

Souvenirs of the Fairs...13

How World's Fairs Began...23

140 Years of World's Fairs...30

From Steam Engines to the Space Age...32

More Expos Are Coming...41

Words You Should Know...46

Index...47

Above: Monorail train and Wonder Wall; Louisiana World Exposition, New Orleans, 1984
Below left: United States Pavilion at the 1958 Universal Exhibition in Brussels, Belgium
Below right: Court of Power at the New York World's Fair 1939-1940

WHAT IS AN EXPO?

Sometimes they're called world's fairs. Sometimes they're called expos. (*Expo* is short for *exposition*.) But what is a world's fair, or expo, like?

Imagine you are strolling through a magic city. Holiday crowds fill broad plazas. Fountains splash and sparkle in sunlight. Bright banners flap in the breeze. Flowers are everywhere. You hear the

5

Above left: Marching band from New Orleans visits the 1982 World's Fair in Knoxville, Tennessee.
Left: Lunar Fountain at the New York World's Fair 1964-1965
Above: Man in the Community, a theme pavilion at Expo 67, Montreal, Canada, 1967

happy sounds of a brass band marching down the street.

All around you are buildings in many different shapes and colors. Some of those buildings—or pavilions—make you think

6

Above: Tower of the Sun. More than 60 million people visited Expo '70, in Osaka, Japan.

you're in another part of the world. Some look so strange, you may think you're on another planet! And everything you see looks brand-new. You're at a world's fair!

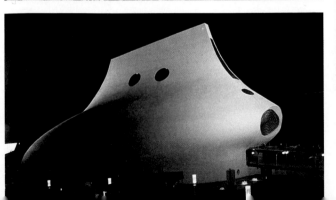

Unusual shapes at Expo '70, Osaka, Japan: Toshiba-IHI Pavilion (above left), Gas Pavilion (left), Switzerland's "Radiant Structure" (above)

Above: Mexican mariachi band entertains visitors at HemisFair '68, San Antonio, Texas, 1968.
Above right: Quebec Pavilion, Expo 67, Montreal
Right: Philippine Pavilion, New York World's Fair 1964-1965

INSIDE THE PAVILIONS

Nations from every continent take part in a big world's fair. In their pavilions, you enjoy music, dancing, art, and handicrafts

1982 World's Fair, Knoxville: Rubik's Cube (left) at the Hungarian Pavilion and dancers at Korean Pavilion (right)

from faraway lands. You learn how people live in other countries. You taste delicious new kinds of food.

Other pavilions represent big companies. They surprise you over and over again. You might see a movie on a screen that completely surrounds you.

9

Industrial robot demonstrates its dexterity in the Italian Pavilion of Expo 67 in Montreal.
Amusement rides are a part of many expos. HemisFair '68, San Antonio, Texas.

Or a 3-D movie that is so
realistic, you feel as if
you're part of the action.
You might see a show
acted by robots.

At some pavilions,
difficult scientific ideas are

explained in ways that

make them easy to
understand—and even fun.
Or you may enjoy a
preview of inventions that
haven't been invented yet!
In another part of the fair,
you can ride a Ferris wheel
or a carousel, or go on a
thrilling roller-coaster ride.

So you could say that
world's fairs or expos are
like science museums, art
galleries, amusement
parks, movie theaters,
concert halls, circuses,
botanical gardens, cities of

the future, and a trip
around the world—all
rolled into one, and with
many things of their own
added.

An expo is a wonderful
place to be—while it lasts.
Most expos are open for
only one six-month
season—from spring to
fall—before being torn
down. A few have run for
two seasons, but no major
expo has lasted longer
than that.

The Eiffel Tower, built for the 1889 Exposition, was part of the 1900 Universal Exposition in Paris, France.

SOUVENIRS OF THE FAIRS

When the fair is gone, however, something may remain as a permanent "souvenir." The Eiffel Tower in Paris, France, is a reminder of the 1889 Exposition. Nothing so tall had ever been built

Left: Still a wonder today: Eiffel Tower.
The pool was part of the 1937
Paris Exposition.
Above: Seattle's Space Needle and
Pacific Science Center were built
for Century 21 Exposition of 1962.

before. But at the time, a
group of angry Parisians
called it "unnecessary and
monstrous."

The Space Needle in
Seattle, Washington, was
built for the 1962
Century 21 Exposition. The

Left: Tower of the Americas was originally part of HemisFair '68 in San Antonio.
Right: Sunsphere was the theme structure of 1982 World's Fair in Knoxville, Tennessee.

Tower of the Americas in
San Antonio, Texas, was
built for HemisFair in 1968.
Knoxville's Sunsphere was
a part of the 1982 World's
Fair.

The Atomium in Brussels,
Belgium, was built for the

Above: Atomium was a theme building for the 1958 Universal Exhibition in Brussels.
Above right: Unisphere, a huge globe of the earth, was built for the New York World's Fair 1964-1965.
Right: Canada Place, in Vancouver's harbor, was the Canada Pavilion at Expo 86.

World's Fair of 1958. It still stands, as does the Unisphere from the New York World's Fair of 1964-1965 and Canada Place, built for Vancouver's Expo 86.
Several buildings that

Left: Exhibit palaces surround South Canal at the 1893 World's Columbian Exposition in Chicago.   Above right: Palace of Fine Arts as it looked at Chicago's 1893 fair and (below) as it looks today, housing the Museum of Science and Industry

were built for world's fairs
have been turned into
museums. For example, the
Museum of Science and
Industry was built for the 1893
World's Columbian Exposition
in Chicago, Illinois.

17

Left: Tower of Jewels at the Panama-Pacific International Exposition, San Francisco, 1915.   Above: San Francisco's 1915 Palace of Fine Arts is now the Exploratorium, a science museum.

San Francisco's Palace of Fine Arts, which now houses the Exploratorium science museum, was part of the 1915 Panama-Pacific Exposition. Seattle's Science Center came from Century 21, and the Queens

Museum in New York City dates from the 1939-1940 World's Fair.

Many public buildings remain in San Diego's Balboa Park from two expositions, held in 1915-1916 and 1935-1936. In

One of the Spanish Colonial style buildings in San Diego's Balboa Park

Below: New York City's Flushing Meadow Corona Park was the site of world's fairs in 1939-1940 and 1964-1965.

Habitat was built as part of Expo 67. It showed visitors a new way of constructing apartment houses.

Montreal, Canada, people live in Habitat, which was built for Expo 67. Each separate apartment in the complex was built on the ground and then lifted into place by a giant crane.

Many parks also were once part of a world's fair. Fairmount Park was the

20

Festive fairgoers throng Chicago's 1893 World's Columbian Exposition, which celebrated the 400th anniversary of Columbus' discovery of America.

site of Philadelphia's 1876 Centennial Exposition. Jackson Park, Chicago, was home to the 1893 Columbian Exposition.

Often an area must be transformed so that a world's fair can be held there. A trash dump in Queens was changed

21

Left: Trylon and Perisphere was the theme center
of the New York World's Fair 1939-1940,
called the "World of Tomorrow."   Above: Exotic
architecture on Treasure Island in San
Francisco Bay was a feature of the
Golden Gate International Exposition,
1939-1940. Later, Treasure Island
became a naval base.

for New York City's two
world's fairs in 1939-1940
and 1964-1965. Today,
it is known as Flushing
Meadow Corona Park.
Treasure Island was created
for the Golden Gate
International Exposition of
1939-1940 in San Francisco.

HOW WORLD'S FAIRS BEGAN

The first true world's fair was held in 1851. But there were fairs of a sort for more than a thousand years before that. Those early fairs were really markets.

Farmers, merchants, and craft workers would meet at the same time every year in certain towns along busy trade routes to show and sell their wares.

A fair in France, 13th century

These fairs were the only
opportunity that many
people had to buy goods
from distant places, such
as spices from the Far East.
Important fairs were held
in England, France, Russia,
and other countries.

In 1849, Henry Cole, a British government official, proposed a daring idea: Why not hold an international exhibition in London? All the nations of the world could be invited to display products from their farms, forests, and mines; their manufactured goods; their latest machines and vehicles; their arts and crafts.

Cole's plan was eagerly supported by Prince Albert,

Prince Albert and Queen Victoria

the husband of Queen
Victoria. With Albert's
support, the planners of
the exhibition were able to
raise the necessary funds.

The Crystal Palace, a
single glass-and-iron
building in Hyde Park,
housed almost all the
exhibits for this first world's
fair. Nothing like the Crystal
26 Palace had ever been built

Joseph Paxton

before. Designed by Joseph Paxton, it looked something like a greenhouse, but it was much, much bigger than any greenhouse.

The Crystal Palace was a prefabricated building. It was made of standardized units—including almost 300,000 panes of glass— that were made in factories, then brought to Hyde Park and fitted into place. At a

Above: The first world's fair was held
at the Crystal Palace in London, England, in 1851.
Left: Interior of the Crystal Palace

time when most public
buildings were made of
stone, the Crystal Palace
was so light and airy that
some Londoners were
afraid it would collapse!
On May 1, 1851, Queen

Victoria formally opened the Great Exhibition of the Works of Industry of All Nations. And the crowds came!

Visitors marveled at the latest in steam-powered machinery, the new art of photography, and other displays from forty nations. When the Crystal Palace closed its doors in October, over 6 million people had visited the fair. The queen herself loved the exhibition and went there often.

140 YEARS OF WORLD'S FAIRS

The success of the London exhibition inspired other cities to hold expositions, large and small. Paris has held the most fairs, eight of them between 1855 and 1937—but none since. Expo '70 in Osaka, Japan, set an attendance record with 60 million visitors.

Expos help people keep up with changes. They also

Top left: Nighttime magic; Tower of the Sun at San Francisco's Golden Gate International Exposition, 1939-1940.   Top right: Huge sculpture by Alexander Calder was displayed at Montreal's Expo 67.   Bottom left: Space exploration exhibit, United States Pavilion, at Expo '70 in Osaka, Japan. Bottom right: French Pavilion at Expo 67, Montreal.

provide a look into the future. Expos present new inventions, new methods of transportation, and new styles of buildings, art, and entertainment.

31

FROM STEAM ENGINES TO THE SPACE AGE

Try to imagine how visitors at the 1876 Centennial Exposition in Philadelphia, Pennsylvania, felt when they saw the giant 1,500-horsepower Corliss engine in action! What did they think about a new invention called the telephone, or the first practical typewriter?

Many communities did not yet have electricity in 1893. No wonder people

Left: President Grant starts up the Corliss engine to open the 1876 Centennial Exposition, Philadelphia. Above: Great Basin of the World's Columbian Exposition, Chicago, 1893. Visitors were dazzled by the effects of electric lights.

were so impressed by the way the Columbian Exposition in Chicago was lit up at night. Only one "horseless carriage" was shown there. But eleven years later, visitors could admire 160 automobiles at

Two views of the Louisiana Purchase Exposition held in St. Louis, Missouri in 1904. This fair is celebrated in the song "Meet Me in St. Louis, Louis."

the Louisiana Purchase Exposition in St. Louis.

The main buildings at those two world's fairs were based on styles hundreds of years old. But they were considered the last word in beauty and elegance by

most fairgoers of the time.

Above left: Aquacade, spectacular music-and-swimming show, at New York World's Fair 1939-1940
Bottom left: Federal (United States) Building at the Century of Progress Exposition, in Chicago, 1933-1934
Above: Travel and Transport Building at Chicago's Century of Progress

In 1933-1934, forty years after the Columbian Exposition, the Century of Progress was held in Chicago—and it looked entirely different. The architects who designed the buildings wanted them to be simpler, less cluttered with decoration, and "streamlined" like the latest passenger planes or racing cars. This "modern" style is called Art Deco today.

The New York World's Fair of 1939-1940 was called the World of Tomorrow. A tall spire and a huge globe, the Trylon and the Perisphere, made up its "theme center." Visitors thrilled to their first look at television and rode on moving chairs to view

General Motors Building (left) at New York World's Fair 1939-1940. Visitors rode moving chairs (above) to view the Futurama, a vast scale model of what America might look like in 1960.

the Futurama, a scale model of what America might look like in the distant future—1960! Both 1939-1940 fairs, New York's and San Francisco's, were magic lands at night, transformed by spectacular new lighting techniques.

Night lighting and the futuristic Sumitomo Pavilion
at Expo '70, Osaka, Japan

Space exploration also
has been featured. In 1958,
the Soviet Union showed a
model of *Sputnik*, the first
artificial satellite, at the
Brussels World's Fair. At
Expo '70, in Osaka, Japan, the
United States displayed an

A great thrill in 1893: Engineer George W. Ferris' giant wheel (left) at the World's Columbian Exposition, Chicago, Illinois. A 1986 thrill: the Scream Machine (right) at Expo 86, Vancouver, Canada

actual rock from the moon.

World's fairs have a lighter side, too. Starting with the Midway at the World's Columbian Exposition in 1893, most fairs have had amusement parks. The star attraction of the Midway was the

first Ferris wheel. Ice cream
cones were "invented" at
the St. Louis fair in 1904.
Walt Disney created several
rides and shows for the New
York World's Fair of 1964-1965,
including "It's a Small World."

Ice cream cones were still a world's fair
treat in 1970 at Osaka, Japan. Walt Disney's
"It's a Small World" (above) was created for the
New York World's Fair 1964-1965.

MORE EXPOS ARE COMING

World's fairs, with their blend of fact, fantasy, and the future, are as popular as ever. The last four international expositions— Expo '85 in Tsukuba, Japan; Expo 86 in

"Far-out" architecture at Expo '85, Tsukuba, Japan: Gas Pavilion (below) and Sumitomo Pavilion, an optical illusion (right). Part of the yellow cube is actually a reflection in the pavilion's mirrored facade.

Above left: Expo Centre, theme pavilion at Expo 86,
Vancouver, Canada, 1986
Above right: Fujitsu Pavilion at Expo '90 in Osaka, Japan, 1990
Below left: Hitachi Pavilion at Expo '90
Below center: "Human factor" sculptures like these amused
visitors to World Expo 88, Brisbane, Australia, 1988.
Right: Maori dancer, New Zealand Pavilion
at World Expo 88, in Brisbane

Vancouver, Canada; World Expo 88 in Brisbane, Australia; and Expo '90 in Osaka, Japan—all drew great crowds.

Expos are often held to celebrate important anniversaries. Philadelphia's 1876 Centennial Exposition marked 100 years of American independence. The 500th anniversary of the discovery of America by Christopher Columbus will be celebrated by Expo '92 in Seville, Spain.

Above: United States Science Pavilion at Seattle's 1962 Century 21 Exposition. Today it is a museum, the Pacific Science Center. Right: Expo Oz was the platypus mascot of World Expo 88, in Brisbane, Australia.

Expo '92 has more countries taking part in it than any exposition ever held, and more world's fairs are being planned. Expo 2000, scheduled to take place in Hannover, Germany, will mark the end of the 20th century. Maybe you will have a chance to visit a great expo someday. If you do, you're sure to have an exciting, unforgettable time!

Above: Highway 86 sculpture, a rippling roadway
with over 200 vehicles, at Expo 86,
Vancouver, Canada
Right: Ships of the world at Expo 86, which had a
transportation and communications theme

WORDS YOU SHOULD KNOW

artificial (ar • tih • FISH • il) — made by people; not natural

botanical (boh • TAN • ih • kil) — having to do with the growing and study of trees, flowers, and other plants

continent (KAHN • tih • nent) — a large landmass on the earth

elegance (EL • ih • gence) — the quality of being rich-looking and attractive in a tasteful way

galleries (GAL • er • eez) — rooms where artworks are displayed to the public

greenhouse (GREEN • howss) — a building with glass or clear plastic walls and roof, used for growing plants

horsepower (HORSS • pow • er) — a unit for measuring the power of an engine; derived from comparing the engine's power to the pulling power of a horse

international (in • ter • NASH • uh • nil) — between nations; coming from many different nations

invention (in • VEN • shun) — a new machine or a new way of doing something

monstrous (MAHN • struss) — different from the normal; freakish; outlandish

obstacle (AHB • stih • kil) — anything that gets in the way of progress; difficulty

official (uh • FISH • il) — a person who holds a position of authority; a member of a government department

opportunity (ahp • er • TOO • nih • tee) — a chance to do something

ornate (or • NAYT) — highly decorated

pavilion (pah • VIL • yun) — a building used for exhibits at a fair

plaza (PLAH • za) — an open area in a city or town, usually surrounded by buildings

practical (PRAK • tih • kil) — useful; able to accomplish a task easily and cheaply

prefabricated (pre • FAB •rih • kayt • ed) — having parts put together in a factory so that construction consists of assembling the preformed parts

realistic (re •uh • LISS • tik) — like real life; like things really are

robot (ROH • baht) — a machine that is made to imitate the actions of a human being

satellite (SAT • ih • lyt) — a body that revolves around a heavenly body, such as a planet

souvenir (soo • ven • EER) — an object kept to remind someone of something; a memento

spire (SPYR) — a tall structure that comes to a point at the top, like a church steeple

standardized (STAN • der • dyzed) — made alike; made after the same pattern

streamlined (STREEM • lyned) — having a shape that allows easy movement through air or water

technique (tek • NEEK) — a way of using materials and tools to do or make something

theme (THEEM) — the main topic or subject; the main idea

transportation — any means of traveling, or of carrying something, from one place to another

INDEX

architecture, 6-7, 20, 26-28, 31, 34-36
art, 8, 11, 31
Art Deco, 36
Atomium, 15
automobiles, 33-34
Balboa Park, 19
Brussels, Belgium, 15, 38
Canada Place, 16
Centennial Exposition (1876), 21, 32, 43
Century of Progress, 35
Century 21 Exposition, 14, 18

Chicago, 17, 21
Cole, Henry, 25
Columbian Exposition
Corliss engine, 32
Crystal Palace, 26-29
dancing, 8
Disney, Walt, 40
Eiffel Tower, 13-14
electricity, 32
Exploratorium, 18
Expo 67 (Montreal, Canada), 20
Expo '70 (Osaka, Japan), 30, 38
Expo '85 (Tsukuba, Japan), 41

Expo 86 (Vancouver, Canada), 16, 41-43
Expo 88 (Brisbane, Australia), 43
Expo '90 (Osaka, Japan), 43
Expo '92 (Seville, Spain), 43-44
Expo 2000 (Hannover, Germany), 44-45
Fairmount Park, 20-21
fairs, early, 23-24
Ferris wheel, 11, 39-40
flowers, 5, 11
Flushing Meadow Corona Park, 22

food, 9
fountains, 5
Futurama, 37
Golden Gate International
    Exposition, 22
Habitat, 20
handicrafts, 8
HemisFair, 15
ice cream cones, 40
inventions, 11
Jackson Park, 21
Knoxville, Tennessee, 15
London, England, 25
Louisiana Purchase Exposition
    (1904), 34, 40
Midway, 39
Montreal, Canada, 20
movies, 9-10, 11
Museum of Science and Industry,
    17
museums, 17, 18-19
music, 6, 8, 11
New York City, 16, 19, 22
New York World's Fair (1939), 36,
    37
New York World's Fair (1964), 40
Palace of Fine Arts, 18
Panama-Pacific Exposition, 18
Paris, France, 13, 30
parks, 20-22

pavilions, 6-7, 8, 9, 10
Paxton, Joseph, 27
Perisphere, 36
Philadelphia, 21, 32, 43
plazas, 5
Prince Albert, 25-26
Queen Victoria, 26, 29
rides, 11
robots, 10
San Antonio, 15
San Diego, 19
San Francisco, 18, 37
scientific ideas, 10-11
seasons of expos, 12
Seattle, Washington, 14, 18
Soviet Union, 38
Space Needle, 14
Sputnik, 38
Sunsphere, 15
telephone, 32
television, 36
Tower of the Americas, 15
Treasure Island, 22
Trylon, 36
typewriter, 32
Unisphere, 16
World of Tomorrow, 36
World's Columbian Exposition
    (1893), 17, 21, 33, 35, 39

About the Author

Allan Fowler is a free-lance writer with a background in advertising. Born in New York, he lives in Chicago now and enjoys traveling. He has visited every important expo since the New York World's Fair of 1964-1965.